P9-BZR-152

Chi's Sweet Home

チーズ スイートホーム

8

Konami Kanata

contents

homemade 129~146+

129 a cat manifests 3

130 a cat anticipates 11

131 a cat cases 19

132 a cat is wowed 27

133 a cat has a blast 35

134 a cat is pursued 43

135 a cat is hemmed 51

136 a cat leaps 59

137 a cat returns 67

138 a cat relaxes 75

139 a cat monitors 83

140 a cat steps out 91

141 a cat infiltrates 99

142 a cat judges 107

143 a cat attempts 115

144 a cat concerns 123

145 a cat reconnects 131

146 a cat sheds tears 139

Let's Make a Chi Face 147

homemade 129: a cat manifests

SWIFF
PLOP
RISE
SWIP
SWIP
SWIP
MEOW
SPROING
SWIFF
SMAK
SLIP
FIP
SLUMP
WHUMP

TRY NOT TO GET IN MY WAY, CHI.
MIYA
MIYA
MOMMY, CHI WANTS TO PLAY TOO!
BOING
BONG
I'M DOING SOME CLEANING.
SWIP
MIYA
BUT CHI CAN'T REACH.
OH!
SWIP
SWIP
WOAH!
I CAN REACH FROM UP THERE.
HOP
HOP
HOP
GRIN

OH-NO-O
SWIP
SWIP
JUST A LITTLE MORE!
MUFU
HUH?
CLOOP
AH ...
EEK!
MEOWR

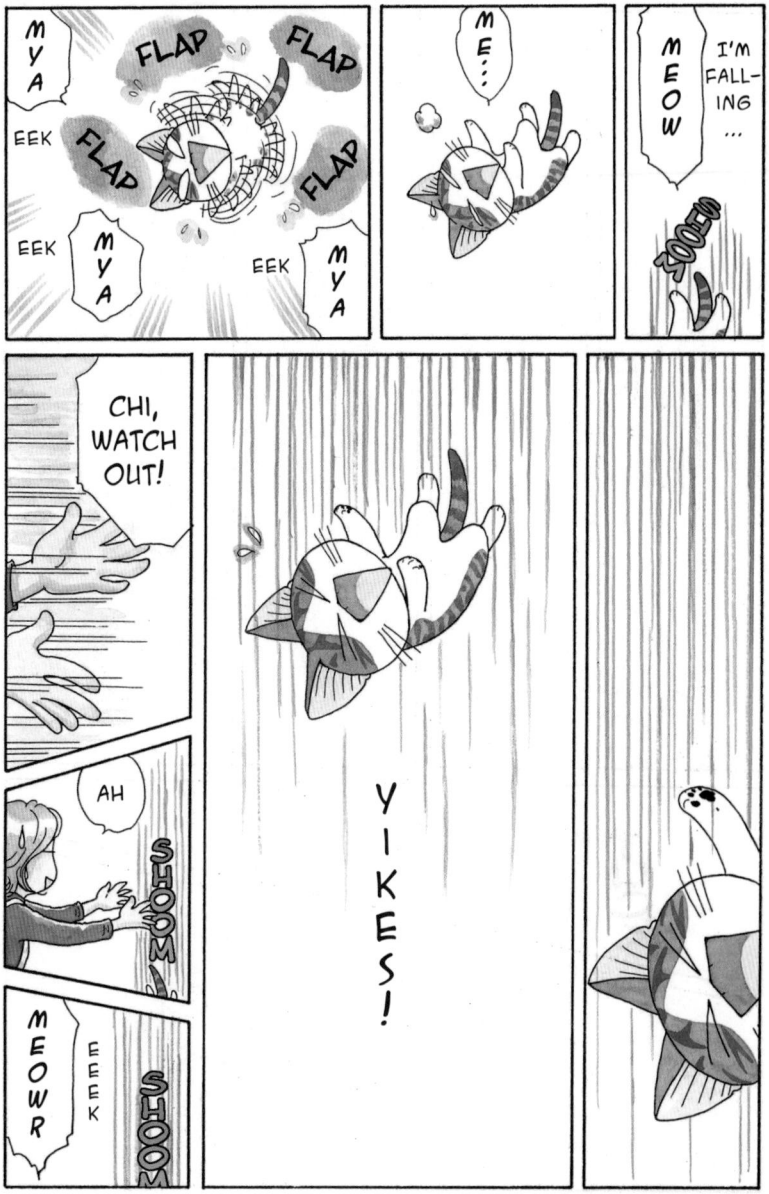
MEOW
I'M FALLING ...
SHOOK
ME...
MYA
FLAP
FLAP
EEK
FLAP
FLAP
EEK
MYA
EEK
MYA
YIKES!
CHI, WATCH OUT!
AH
SHOOM
MEOWR
EEEK
SHOOM

TUCK

FLIP

SHOMP
WOW
MEOW
AWE-SOME!
CHI, AREN'T YOU AMAZING!
I DON'T KNOW, BUT THAT WAS AMAZING!
MEOW

the end

homemade 130: a cat anticipates

BUSTL
BUSTL
BUSTL
BUSTL
MIYA
MOMMY, WE GONNA PLAY?
CRUN-CHIES?
I HAVE SOME LEFT.
KRUNCH
KRUNCH
KRUNCH
FLUT
FLUT
FLUT
DADDY, CAN WE PLAY?!
MIYA
DASH—
AREN'T YOU SO SPOILED, CHI.
NUNNL
NUNNL
TMP TMP....

I WONDER IF HE'S OUT THERE?
CHI'LL BE BACK!
MEOW
LOP
IS HE, IS HE?
MYA
MYA

...
DITHER
HITHER THITHER
IS HE?
IS HE?
AHH...
HAH
HAH
HA

HE IS!
HEY HEY!
MEOW MEOW
HEYYY!
MEOW
DASH
COCCHI!
MEOW
MIYA
I KNEW YOU'D BE HERE!
HA
HA

MEOW
CHI KNEW SHE'D FIND YOU HERE.
DID COCCHI THINK SO, TOO?
MYA
MRR
TSK
MRR
I JUST HAPPENED TO PASS BY.
MRR
SO IS YOUR STOMACH BETTER?
HUH?
MYA
MIYA
HOW'D YOU KNOW?
MRR
I AIN'T TELLING...
MIYA
WHA?
MRR
SO...
MERR
WHAT DO YA WANT FROM ME?
MEOW
LET'S PLAY!

MRR
TSK.
I AIN'T PLAYING.
MERRR
MIYA
WHAT?
SPRING
MIYA
LET'S PLAY ...
MIYA
WHY, WHY?
MRR
I'M BUSY ...
MRR
I JUST AM.
TIP TIP TIP...
TIP TIP TIP...
MRR
LATER.
TIPTIPTIP...
...
HMM ?
MEOW
WHAZZAT ?
WHOA!
MEOW
MEOW
YEAH!

MYAMYA
RSTL
RSTL
RSTL
RSTL
STAR
STAR
STAR

homemade 131: a cat cases

BUT CHI WAS PLAYING WITH IT.
MEOW
MRR
HOW NAIVE.
HUH?
MRR
YOU HAVEN'T CHECKED WHAT'S INSIDE?
!
MYA
MYA
C-CHI WAS THINKING TO.
MERRR
REALLY?
MEOW
IT MIGHT BE SOMETHING AWESOME.
MEOW
YEAH, SOMETHING AWESOME.
MRR
AWESOME?
MRR
AWESOME... LIKE WHAT?
HUH?
MYA

AWE-SOME...
LIKE...
MILK
MEOW
DO YOU GET IT, COCCHI?
MRR
HRN ?
AWESOME, THAT'S LIKE...
MRR
LET'S JUST CHECK IT OUT.
MRR
WHAT COULD IT BE?
MYA
MRR
SUSPI-CIOUS ...

I CAN'T SEE ALL THE WAY IN...
MRR
MEOW
NOPE.
MRR
I'M GONNA CHECK.
MEOW
CHI'S GOING FIRST.
SHUV
PLUSH

MEOW
SOME-THING'S IN THERE!
ALL RIGHT!
MERR
IT WAS PLUSHY.
MYA
WHAT IS IT?
MYA MYA
MRR MRR
IT'S AWE-SOME!
RUMAGE
RUMAGE
RUMAGE
PLUSH
MRR
THERE IT IS—
HUH?

...
BIKKURI
MRR
OUCH!
...
...
...
MEOW
HUH, IT WAS JUST COCCHI'S PAW.
MRR
TSK, IT WAS JUST YOU.
MRR
WE STRUCK OUT.
CHUNZ PARK
MIYA
WHAT DO WE DO NEXT?
MRR
HUH ?!

MRR
I'M BUSY!
MYA
REALLY?
MIYA
WHERE YA GOING?
MRR
WHO KNOWS!
HALT
HALT
SUSPICIOUS!
MIYA
WHAT'S THAT?
MRR
MEOW
WHAT, WHAT?

MERR
MEOW
SQU EEZ
MOVE OVER, COCCHI!
MEOW
MRR
YOU'RE IN THE WAY!
MUSH
SQUEEZE
ICK

the end

MEOW
MEOW
MRR
IN MY WAY!
MRR
GOOMPH
GOOMPH
I'LL GO IN FIRST!
MRR
MEOW
CHI'S FIRST.
MEOW
CHI IS!
SMAR
OUCH!
MRR
I AM!
MRR
DOOF
MYA
-NOS!

MEOW
MOVE
MRR
IN MY WAY!
MRR
WHAT?!
MEOW
STOP!
IT'S NO GOOD.
MEOW
MRR
LET'S DO THIS AGAIN.
TAP
TAP
WE CAN'T GO THROUGH TOGETHER.
MIYA
MRR
LOOKS LIKE IT.
MRR
WE'VE GOTTA GO THROUGH ONE BY ONE.
YUP, YOU'RE RIGHT.
MRR
SQU EEZ
CHI'S GOING IN FIRST!
MEOW
MRR
MERR
NO, I AM!
OF COURSE I'M GOING FIRST!

MYA
HUH? WHY "OF COURSE"?

WHY, WHY?
MIYA
MRR
W-WELL ...

MRR...
THAT'S BE-CAUSE...

GADE

MERR
A SCARY THING MIGHT APPEAR.

MYA
CHI'S ISN'T SCARED OF ANY-THING.

OH ...

HIKKOSHI

...
SNIB
HEH HEH
MRR
I'LL GO ON AHEAD THEN.
MIYA
COCCHI, ARE YOU OKAY?
COME ON OVER.
MRR
NASH

MIYA
MRR
ALREADY SCARED, HUH?
MIYA
THERE AREN'T ANY SCARY THINGS?
I WONDER ...
MRR
SMIRK
MRR
LET'S GO.
MRR
SO SUSPICIOUS ...
SLINK SLINK
NO SCARY THINGS, PLEASE!
SLINK

SLINK
SNAP
EEEK
MEOW
WOAH
MERRG
BOI-NG
BOI-NG
R
WH-WHAT IS IT?
MRR
MYA...
SOME-THING SNAPPY —
MYA
HERE.
MRR
HUH?
MEOW
PHEW, WHAT A RELIEF.
MRR
HOW COULD YOU BE AFRAID OF THAT?

MRR
WHAT'S BACK THERE?
SNEAK
SNEAK
NOTHING SCARY, PLEASE.
MEOW
SLINK SLINK
SLINK
YOW
BOING
MEOWR
EEEK
WHOA
MERRR
SADDLE
MRR
WHAT NOW?
MERR
HOW COULD GRASS FRIGHTEN YOU?

the end

homemade 133: a cat has a blast

MEOW
SO BRIGHT.
MYSTERIOUS...
MRR...

MRR
THE LEAVES ARE RUSTLING.
MYA
IT'S DARK.
STARE
MRR
OY! THERE'S SOMETHING HERE!
NASH
MYA
REALLY? WHAT?
MRR
COME ALONG, CHI.
SHAK SHAK SHAK
MEOW
IS IT SAFE, COC-CHI?
NASH

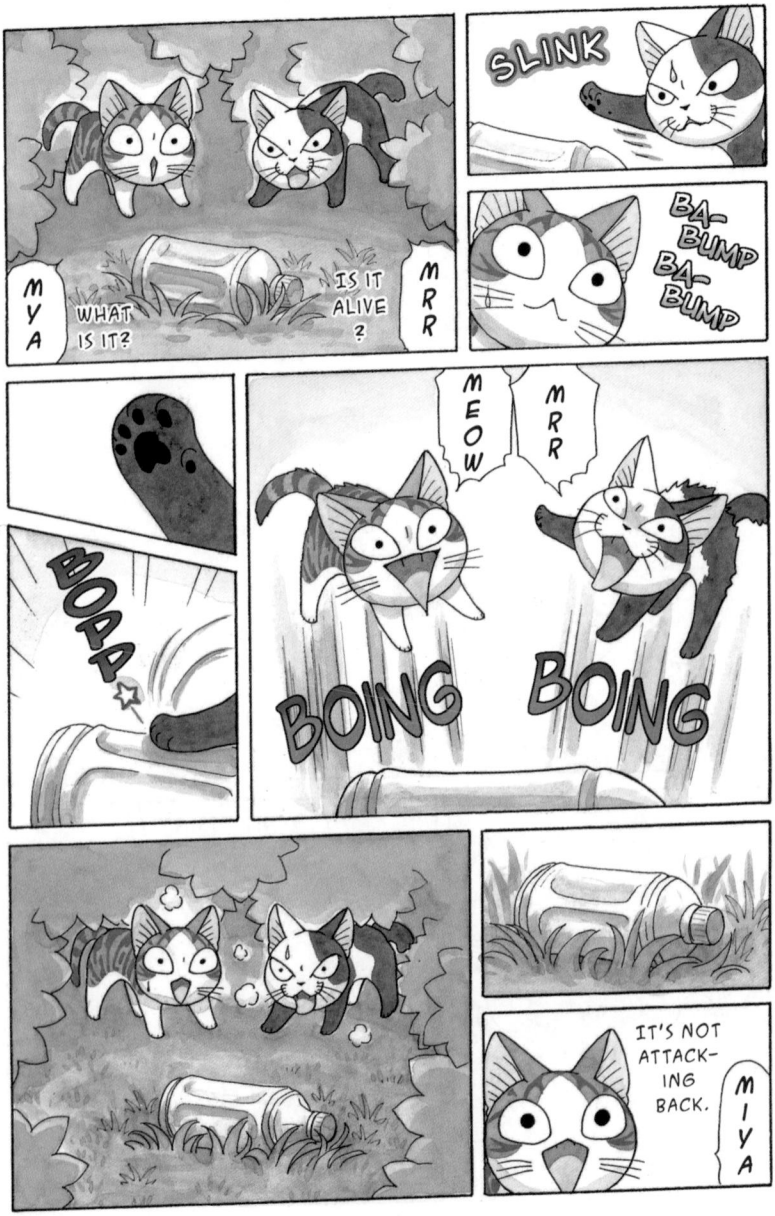
MYA
WHAT IS IT?
IS IT ALIVE?
MRR
SLINK
BA-BUMP BA-BUMP
BOPP
MEOW
MRR
BOING
BOING
IT'S NOT ATTACKING BACK.
MIYA

THEN CHI'S GONNA BOP IT, TOO!
MEOW
BOP BOP BOP
SNIF SNIF
MRR
IT'S NOT ALIVE AND IT'S NOT FOOD, EITHER.
MRR
WHAT COULD IT BE?
IT MUST BE FOR BOPPING!
MEOW
SEE?
MEOW
BOP BOP BOP BOP BOP BOP BOP BOP
MRR
I GUESS SO.
NAIOI
NAIOI
NAIOI
NAIOI
THERE'S SOME-THING HERE!
MEOW

MRR
WHAT THE HECK?
SUSPICIOUS ...
MRR
MEOW
DEFINITELY.
MEOW
WHAT COULD IT BE?
REACH
GRIP
TUG
MYA
HUH ?
SLOTH
SLAK

SLOP
MEOWR
YIKES!!
WHOA!
MERRR
MRR
RUN AWAY!
SCARY THING!!
MEOW
DASH
NHAK!

OZZEOW
OZZEOW
THWUMP
HUH
HUH
HUH
HUH
HUH
HUH
HUH
HUH
THAT WAS FUN.
MEOW

the end

homemade 134: a cat is pursued

MEOW
CHI'S REALLY FAST!
SKOOT——
MERR
I'M WAY FASTER!
SKOOT—
MEOW
CHI'S EVEN FASTER!
DASH

MEOW
SEE?
SKOOT

RUFF
!

MEOW
EEK EEK EEK !

MRR
HEH, IT'S JUST A DOG.

WHA?
HMPH

YOU SEE... A DOG'S GOT A LEASH,
MRR
SO IT CAN'T MOVE FREELY.
MRR
MRR
TUT, TUT.
PAT-PAT
TUG
MEOW
AH-HAH.
MEOW
SEE?
MRR
COCCHI SURE KNOWS A LOT.
BOUND
OH!

RUFF
DASH
FRSK
!
!
MEOWR
YIKES!
MRRR
RUN, CHI!
MEOR
EEK! OH NOS!
DASH——
SNAP
MYA
OH, RIGHT!
MYA
LET'S HIDE!
MRR
HIDE?
MEOW
BLACKIE SHOWED ME HOW.

MEOR
IF WE HIDE QUIETLY.
MRR
WILL WE BE OKAY HERE?
ISSN
MERR
IT NEVER LOST US, DUMMY.
MEOR
IT'S FOUND US!
SLAK
SLAK
RUFF
SLAK
!
RUFF
RUFF
RUFF
RUFF
RUN AWAY!
MEOR
RUN!
MERR
DASH

MRR
RUN, CHI!
MEOR
EEK!
DASH—
TROT
TROT
TROT
MEERR
FOLLOW ME, CHI!
MHEOW
I CAN'T RUN ANYMORE...
!

MERR
CHI, JUMP!
WHAT ?!
JUMP !
MERR
TAZO
GRIP

!
MEOW
COCCHI !
PHEW
MEYOWW
BWAAH
MRR
YOU COULDN'T JUMP ANY HIGHER?!

the end

homemade 135: a cat is hemmed
YIPE!
RUFF RUFF
FSSK
STAY AWAY!
FSSK
DON'T COME NEAR ME!

SKEE
MERR
CHI, HURRY UP AND CLIMB!
LICK
SKEE
SKEE
SKEE
MEGOWR
SKAT
!

MRR...
CH-CHI, YOU ARE FAST!
HA
HA
HA
STOP THAT.
YAP
YAP
MEW
MEW
MEW
MEOW
WE'RE SAFE.
MRR
HUH?
MM-ZZ
MM-ZZ
MM-ZZ
HEY, YOU...
MRR
MII
HMM?

MEOW
CHI SMELLS LIKE DOG!
SNIFF
SNIFF
SNIFF
WHA ?
?!
SMELL LIKE DOG!
MRR!

LICK
LICK
LICK
LICK
LICK
LICK

MRR
IT'S CUZ THAT DOG LICKED YOU JUST NOW.
MEOW
BUT COCCHI SMELLS LIKE DOG TOO!
!
MRR
YOU GOT IT ON ME.
MEOW
YOU SMELL WEIRD!

MIYA
I CAN'T REACH ...

MRR
WHAT CAN YOU DO...
LICK
LICK
LICK

MRR
YOU MEAN "SORRY."
MYA
THANK YOU.

LICK LICK LICK LICK LICK LICK LICK LICK

ALL RIGHT!
MRR

MRR
WE'VE GOT OUR SMELLS BACK!

MEOW
YEAH, WE DID!
NEAT!
MEOW

MYA
RIGHT
YUP
MRR

MEOW
WE'RE UP REALLY HIGH.
REALLY HIGH.
MRR
HOW DO WE GET DOWN?
MRR
IT'S NO USE.
SAY—
MIYA
MEOW
LET'S JUMP OVER THERE.
MRR
WHERE?

MIYA
ON TOP OF THAT WALL.
MRRR!
WHAT?!
MRRR
NO WAY.
MRRR
IT'S TOO NARROW.
MRRR
AND IT'S FAR DOWN.
MEOW
I'M SURE WE'LL BE FINE.
GEH
HUH?!
MRRR
WHY'S THAT?
MEOW
JUST A HUNCH.
HUH?!

MEOW
SOME-HOW, I'M SURE.
MRR
SOME-HOW?
MRR
THAT WON'T DO!

SOME-HOW...

MRR
YOU MIGHT BE RIGHT!

MYA
YEAH!

the end

homemade 136: a cat leaps

MERR
KPZU
WOAH !
MRR
BAM
!
OH!
MERR
I MISSED!
MEOW!
COCCHI !

FLIP
FLIP
THUMP
MRR
HEH HEH!
MRR
A LITTLE MISSTEP BUT I GOT DOWN.
MRR
NOW IT'S YOUR TURN.
MRR
HEY?
...
MRR
WHAT, ARE YOU SCARED?
MRR
GO AHEAD. WITH BOUNCE IN YOUR BODY YOU'LL LAND JUST FINE.

"BOUNCE" IN MY BODY?
BOUNCE ?
WHAT'S "BOUNCE" ?
MIYA
CHI'S GOT NO BOUNCE.
MRR
DON'T BE FOOLISH, YOU DO.
MRR
YOU'RE A CAT, AFTER ALL.
CHI'S NOT A CAT.
MEOW
WHAT?
MEOW!
CHI'S LIKE MOMMY, DADDY AND YOHEY.
MEOW
CHI'S NOT A CAT!
MRR
WHAT SORT OF EXCUSE IS THAT?
MRR
YOU'RE A CAT!

HAVE FAITH, YOU'RE A CAT!
MRRR
MYA
I CAN'T DO IT!
MYA
CHI'S NOT A CAT!
MRRR?
YOU PLAN TO STAY THERE FOREVER?
MYA
NOS.
I'M GOING HOME.
MYA
MRRR
THEN YOU GOTTA JUMP!
MRRR!
JUMP, CHI!
MRRR!
JUMP!
SPRING

CHI'S GOING HOME!
HOME!
CHI IS NOT A CAT!
NING
BUT...
I FEEL ...
LIKE I CAN!

SHU!
UMP
OH!
THAT'S MY BOUNCE!
MERR!
YOU DID IT, CHI!
HOP
SPRONG
SPRONG

the end

homemade 137: a cat returns

YOU'VE GOT BOUNCE, CUZ YOU'RE A CAT!
THAT WAS SOME BOUNCE, CHI!
YOU'RE A CAT!
HMPH!
MEOW
WEIRD!
MEOW
SO WEIRD!
MEOW
I'M NOT!
TIP TIP TIP TIP
CHASE
MEOW
I'M HUNGRY.
MEOW
DASH
BETTER HURRY HOME!
MEOW
I'M HOME!
MEOW
I'M HUNGRY.
MIYA
MOMMY!

SILENCE
HUH ?
MYA
IS NO ONE HOME?
MIYA
IS CHI'S FOOD READY ?
MIYA
GONE
MYA
MY...

MYA
ONLY WATER.
LAP LAP LAP
GONE

MEOW
FOOD, FOOD!
WANDER WANDER WANDER
PIT PAT PIT PAT PIT
ANY WOULD DO.
MEOW

MYA
FOUND SOME!
GRIP
MYA
WHOA
MIYA
THERE MUST BE SOMETHING HERE, RIGHT?
SALTED POTATO CHIPS
HMM ?
TICK
TICK
HM ?
LAP
LAP

HEY ?
HMM ?
SALTED POTATO CHIPS
MYA?
WHAT'S THIS?
SKF SKF
LICK

MEOW
I DON'T WHAT IT IS BUT...

KSH
MEOW
I'M DIGGING IN!
SALTED POTATO CHIPS

BYE, YOHEI.
BYE-BYE.
OKAY
BYE, YOHEI'S MOM.

TMP
TMP
TMP

OH, IT'S CHI.
OH?

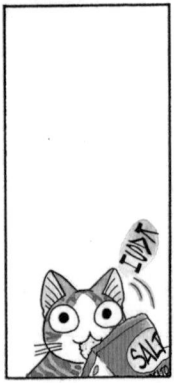
KSH
SALT

HEY, CHI,
THAT'S NOT...
I'M HOME!
WHAT'S WRONG?

CHI! THAT'S —

MEOW
WANNA HAVE SOME, TOO?!
MIYA
THEY'RE GOOD!
SALT
POTATO CHIP

SALTED
LET'S NOT, CHI.
SHOOP

HUH?

SALTED
POTATO CHIPS

WHAT?!

MIYA
HEY, WHY?

NOW HAVE SOMETHING GOOD.

MYA
WOW
NO WORRIES WITH CANNED CAT FOOD.
PHEW
MMIIUU
ONLY FOR CHI!
MMIIUU
I'M SO SPECIAL.
SALT'S NO GOOD FOR CATS.
SNACKS AS A WHOLE.
THIS SALT FLAVOR IS GOOD
YEAH, IT IS TASTY.
...

the end

homemade 138: a cat relaxes

MII?
HRN ?
SUEE
SUEE
MEOW
THIS IS NICE, TOO.
SLLIP...
HEY...
SHOOM
MYA
SO IS THIS.
MEOW
MYA
OH

MEOW
HOP
HOP
HOP
HIGH PLACES ARE GOOD, TOO!
HEH!
MEOW
MEOW
FEELING GOOD!
HEY?
MYA?
MEOW!
WOW!
MIYA
TAP
TAP
TAP
THAT LOOKS GOOD!

SHINE SHINE
MIYA
IT'S SO BRIGHT!
AHH!
MYA
IT'S WARM HERE!
PLOP
MEOW
THIS IS IT!
CHI!
ARGH
WHAT ARE YOU UP TO?
MEOW
YOU'RE IN MY WAY, YOHEY.

MYA
I'M IN YOUR SHADE ...
MYA
YOUR SHADE!
HUH?
WHAT?

AHH

BRIGHT!

IT'S NICE AND WARM HERE.
FLOP

YOHEY AND CHI, THE SAME.

HAH
IT'S WARM AND SNUGGLY.
HAS CHI BEEN ELSE-WHERE ?

SOME-
WHERE
NOT
HERE?
SHIFT
TIP
OH
SQUEEZE

TWITCH
IT SURE IS WARM HERE.
MIU
PURR
PURR
PURR
WHERE WAS THAT?
BUT

the end

homemade 139: a cat monitors

!
MEOW
WHAT IS THAT THING?
WHAT IS IT?
MIYA
WHAT'S IT DOING?
PING
PING
PING
SUFF
SUFF
SUFF
SUFF

PEEK
SKOOT SKOOT SKOOT
MEOW
THERE IT IS!
MEOW
HI THERE!
PING
PING
MIYA
WHATCHA DOING?
PLK
PLK
PLK
PLK
IT'S CLIMBING!
SPRING

WOOSH
IT JUMPED!
!
SMAK
WOW!
RIBBIT
RIBBIT
WHAT'S ITS DEAL?
SNEAK SNEAK SNEAK
RIBBIT

SLINK
OH
MYA
HOP
SLILINK
HEY
MYA
HOP
SHFT
SUSPICIOUS!
TURN

?
!
CROAK
MEOW
DART
MEOW
WAIT!
MEOW
RIBBIT
WAIT UP!
SHIFT
SHK

NOWHERE TO RUN.
SHAK
SHAK
MEOWR
I'VE GOT YA!
WHUM
ZA
SH
RIBBIT
SMISH
MYA?

the end

homemade 140: a cat steps out

CHI LOVES TO PLAY WITH YOHEI.
SHE SURE DOES.
PAT
EVEN IF SHE'S PLAYING HER OWN GAMES.
RUB
RUB
RUB
PURR
PURR
PURR
WANT SOME MILK, CHI?
MILK 3.5
RISE
!

MILK 3.5
MEOW
MOMMY'S GOT MILK!
HOP
DASH—..
MEOW
THANK YOU.
DAD DAD
LAP LAP
DAD DAD
HAHA...
KI-TA KI-TA
KI-TA
AND OUR NEXT STORY IS...
MOORY
MOORY
MRR

MRR
HUH?
THAT VOICE ...
TURN
MRR
CHI—
MRR
COME OUT, CHI!
IT'S COCCHI!
BUT THE MILK...
MRR
COME OUT, CHI.
MRR
CHI!

HM, WHERE'S CHI?
MEOW
BE RIGHT BACK.
MEOW
I'LL HAVE THE MILK LATER.
BOUND
SKOOT

MIYA
WHERE ARE WE GOING?
MRR
SOME PLACE AWESOME!
WHERE? WHERE?
MYA MYA
MRR
IT'S A SECRET.
MIYA
WHAT?
MRR
FOLLOW ME~

MRR
THIS WAY!
HALT
MRR
WE'RE HERE!
MRRR
I'M GONNA MAKE THIS MY SECRET BASE.

the end

homemade 141: a cat infiltrates
OH—
WOW!

YAY!
MEOW
SNIFF
SNIFF
MRR
HAVEN'T I FOUND A COOL PLACE!
TURN
MERRR
WHAT DO YA THINK? HEH HEH!
MIYA
WHERE IS CHI?
MRR
HUH?!
TIZZY
TIZZY

SNEAK
SNEAK
BAM
FOUND YA!
MRR
MYA
EEK!
POP
MEOW
YOU FOUND ME.
MYA
AHH
MRR
OH!
SWA SWA
MEOW
WOW
SNAKE
SNAKE
SNAKE

MEOW
CHI'S GONNA DO THAT TOO!
MRR
YEAH, PULL IT!
TUG TUG
PULL, PULL!
MEOW
WE CAN'T PULL IT ALL, HUH?
MEOW
HAH
HAH~
MRR
MYA
OH
WHAT?
GRIN
SMAK
SMAK

MEOW
LET'S CLIMB!
SKT SKT SKT
SKT SKT SKT
MEOW
CLIMB!
SKT SKT
MEOW
WE'VE CLIMBED IT!
MRR
HEY, IT FLATTENS.
BOF
BOF
MEOW
HEY, THIS IS...
FL
OP
MRR
TSK— WHO CARES ABOUT THAT?
BOUND
MIYA
A GREAT SPOT FOR A NAP!

SHUMP
MRR
HEH HEH... NOW THIS IS IT!
TAP TAP
MRR
I'M MAKING THIS MY NEW SLEEPING PLACE.
CHI'S GOING OVER THERE TOO!
MEOW
ZZZOP
THWAK
SLIDE
MEOW
MINOR FAIL...

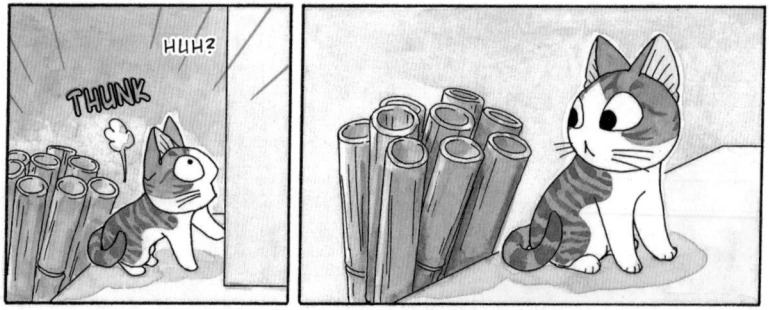
HUH?
THUNK

MEOW
TAKE THAT!

MEOW MEOW
HEAVE HO!
KLANK KLANK

SHOOM

CRASH
KA-KUZO
?!
RATTL RATTL
KOZK
RATTLE
KRASH
RATTL
RATTL
RATTL
RATTL
MEOW
MEOW
MRR
MEOW
I DID IT!
AMAZ-ING!
MRR

the end

homemade 142: a cat judges

MEOW
MEOW
MRR
HRRM ?!
TAKE THIS!
MYA
MRR
IT'S ALL SLIPPY.
SWIP
SWIP
MEOW
THESE SURE WERE A FIND, HUH?
SLIDE
MYA?
WHAT NOW ?
!
UMM!
WHAT !

HEY YOU!
CHI, RUN!
MRR
DART
BOUND
DASH
MEOW
RUN, RUN AWAY!
SKOOT
OH, A DEAD END!
MYA
MEOW
THAT WAY ...
DASH
OH!

SHOO SHOO
YOU PRANK-STER CATS!
SKUOT
OH, BOY.
TURN...
SMILE
WHOA!
WHAT DO I DO?
CLEANERS
MRR
HAH— THAT WAS SURE SCARY, HUH, CHI?
HUFF
HUFF
HUFF
MRR...
CHI ?

PACE
PACE
PACE
PACE
CLE
HUH?
GR IN
I'LL HIDE IN HERE FOR A BIT.
MEOW
THUD THUD
THUD THUD
THUD THUD THUD
COMING THIS WAY...
THUD
THUD

KLONK
KLONK
PEEK
KLONK
KLONK
GRIN
KLONK
KLONK
ONCE I'M ALONE, I'LL SCRAM.
THUMP
THUMP
THUMP...
OH!

TMP
TMP
NOW'S MY CHANCE.
SLINK SLINK
SLIDE
SMAK
HUH?!

WHERE'D THAT CHI RUN OFF TO?
MY SECRET BASE DIDN'T WORK OUT.
MRR
CHI CAN'T GET OUT!

the end

homemade 143: a cat attempts
CHI CAN'T LEAVE.
PACE
PACE
WHAT DO I DO?
WHAT NOW?
PACE
PACE
PACE
MYA
OH RIGHT ...

MEOW
THERE MUST BE ANOTHER WAY OUT.
MYA
HOW ABOUT BACK HERE?
KRAK KRAK
POOF POOF
MYA
CAN'T GET OUT THROUGH HERE.

MYA
HOW ABOUT THAT GAP OVER THERE?
SHA
SHA
SHA
SHA

SHK

THAT NOOK LOOKS SUSPICIOUS.
MYA

MYA
THAT WASN'T IT.

MEOW
IT'S A LITTLE TIGHT.
SUSEEN
SUSEEN
SUSEEN

MEOW
THIS BETTER OPEN UP.
MEOW
IT WON'T ?
SHA
SHA

MEOW
AND THIS SIDE IS NARROW TOO.
NOTSEEN
NOTSEEN

POP
THUD
MYA
THAT WASN'T IT, EITHER.
HAH
MYA
MAYBE UP THERE?
GRIP
OPEN, OPEN!
MYA
MYA
IT WON'T ?
WHERE WILL IT?
MIYA
OH...
MEOW
THIS WAS GONNA BE COCCHI'S "SLEEPING PLACE."
HEH HEH

MYA
I'M GONNA STEP IN.
SHIF
SHIF
SHIF SHIF
NYA NYA
MYA
I'M GONNA REST A BIT.
FLOP
...
AT THIS RATE, THIS WILL BE CHI'S SLEEPING PLACE.
GRRR!
I'M HUNGRY.
GRRR!

MIULK
....
I SHOULD HAVE DRANK IT ALL.
GRRR!
BLOCKS

RISE
GRRR
MEOW
CHI CAN'T BE SLEEPING HERE!

GRIP
MEOW
CHI'S GOING HOME!

HUH ?
MYA

WOAH!
MEOW

MYA
LEAP
THUMP

SLAM

WHAM

KRASH
THUD
THUNK

FOOM
FOOM
FOOM
KOFF
KOFF
KOFF
HAH~
RUB
RUB
RUB
WHAT'S ALL THAT NOISE?
SLIDE
!
OH!

the end

homemade 144: a cat concerns
REACH
!
YOU MED-DLING CAT!

MRR
CHI
HEY, CHI!
MERR
MRR
WHERE ARE YA?
CHI
MRR
MAYBE SHE WENT TO THE PARK?
MRR
TIP TIP
SPLASH
SPLASH
NYU
WELL, I HAVEN'T SEEN HER YET.
NYO
CHI ?

SPLISH
EEEH EEEH
THAT CHI...
HRM
DID SHE DITCH OUR PLAYING AND GO HOME?
MRR
TSK
HOP
MRR
LIKE I CARE ABOUT THAT ONE.
TIP TIP TIP TIP
SHOOM
MRG
WHAT YA DOING, THAT WAS DAN-GEROUS!
KZZ
DUDUDUDUT
DUDUDUD

MRR...
DID SOMETHING HAPPEN TO HER?
SAY, YOHEI ...
IS CHI OVER THERE?
SHE'S NOT WITH ME.
HOW ODD.
WHAT'S UP?
LOOKS LIKE CHI HASN'T COME BACK.
SHE'S BEEN OUT FOR A WHILE.
IT'LL BE NIGHT SOON.
SHE MUST BE HAVING A GOOD TIME THEN, HUH?
HA HA HA

BUT SHE BARELY TOUCHED HER BELOVED MILK...
I LEFT IT OUT FOR HER.
DID SOME-THING HAPPEN TO HER?
UH LIKE WHAT?
LIKE SHE CAN'T COME HOME?
YUP
IS SHE LOST?
HITHER THITHER
THAT MIGHT BE IT.
MAYBE SHE FOL-LOWED SOME-ONE,
OR WAS PICKED UP?
MEOW
FLOP
CHI'S TRUST-ING.
AND SO CUTE.
PROUD

ALSO ...
THERE ARE SO MANY DANGERS OUTDOORS FOR CATS.
DAN-GERS ?
SHE COULD CLIMB UP HIGH AND GET STUCK.
SHE COULD BE HURT AND UNABLE TO MOVE.
THERE ARE RIVERS AND DITCHES.
AND ...
AND ?
LOOOM
BUUUS
SKREE
SKREEE
CHI
LET'S GO LOOK FOR CHI!

CHI!
CHI!
GLARE
GRIT
MEOWR
POUZA
SHOOM
WHIP
DASH

MRR
CHI
MRR
CHI
MRR
CHI
M...
CH...
DASH
MRR!
CHI!
!
MEOW
COCCHI
MEOW
CHI'S ESCAPE: SUCCESS!
MRR
WHAT HAP-PENED TO YOU?
HUEE
HUEE
HUEE

the end

homemade 145: a cat reconnects
WHERE ARE YOU?
CHI
ARE YOU STUCK?
SHAK
SHAK
SHAK
CHI
VROOM
OR RUN OVER?

CHI
WE HAVE NO CLUE...
WHEN CHI GOES OUT...
WHERE DOES SHE GO?
WHAT DOES SHE DO?
YOU SAID IT.

CHI
WHERE ARE YOU?
PANT PANT PANT
SO WHERE'D YOU GO OFF TO?
MRR
MRR
I WAS WORRIED!
I DIDN'T GO OFF ANYWHERE.
MEOW
MRR
AND HOW DID YA GET SO DIRTY?
MICH MICH MICH

MIYA
HUH?
MYA
REALLY?
MRR
DID YA STUMBLE INTO SOME HOLE?!

MEOW
NO WAY!
MRR
WOAH
BAM
HOP
UGH
MEOW
RUN AWAY!
DASH—
MRR
MY TURN!
BLAM
MYA
HOP
WHOA
MRR
WHAM
MEOW
DON'T BLAM INTO ME.
HOP
MEOW
YAY, RUN!
MEOW
I'M GOING HOME!
DASH—
MRR
YOUR HOME ISN'T THAT WAY.
MIYA
WHAT?
CAW
CAW
CAW
CHI
WHERE ARE YOU?
CHI
HOW MUCH TERRITORY CAN A KITTEN COVER ON HER OWN?
CHI
CHI WHERE ARE YOU NOW?

CHI
LOPE
LOPE
LOPE
OH
NYU
LOPE
LOPE
...
IT'S CHI!
HUH ?
OH!

MRR
TAKE THAT.
EEK
MYA
YAR
MYA
WOAH
MRR
IT IS CHI!
AND SHE'S WITH ANOTHER KITTEN.
CHI KNOWS HOW TO GET HOME NOW.
MEOW
MRR
HEH HEH, SO LONG, THEN.
LIOP
SKOOT
DASH!
GRIN
MEOW
SEE YOU TOMORROW.
MEOW
LATER, COCCHI.
MRR!
YEAH!

GOING HOME
MYA
TO MY MILK!

AHHH

HEY, CHI!
CHI!

WOW!

CHI

MEOW
MEOW
DASH
MEOW
EVERY-ONE, I'M BACK!
LET'S HAVE SOME MILK!

THANK GOOD-NESS.
I'M GLAD FOR YOU.
PLUS
CHI'S DIRTY.

MEOW
MIULK
MEOW
MIULK
TMP TMP TMP
MEOW
CHI STILL HAD MIULK LEFT, RIGHT?
OK, READY?
YUP
HUH?
HEY?
KLCK

MIU MIU MIU MIU...
M-I-U-L-K!!
MEOWR
FSSH
GEOWR
FSSH
MEOWR
WHERE DID SHE GET SO DIRTY?
I WONDER WHAT SHE WENT TO GO PLAY.
SSSH
SPLISH
...

the end

homemade 146: a cat sheds tears

DROOP

UH HER LEFT EYE IS ALL DROOPY WITH TEARS.
IS SHE OKAY?
DID SHE GET HURT WHILE SHE WAS OUT?
DOES YOUR EYE HURT?

WE'LL TAKE HER TO THE VET TOMORROW!

KITA D VETERINARY HOSPITAL
MEOW
MEO

LOOKS LIKE CONJUNCTIVITIS.
MEOW

MEOW
CONJUNCTIVITIS?!
OKAY, WE'RE DONE.
IS SHE OKAY?

PINKEYE CAN BE CAUSED BY BACTERIA OR COLDS
BUT IN HER CASE,
DUST AND GRIME SEEM TO HAVE BROUGHT IT ON.

LET'S TRY EYEDROPS FOR A FEW DAYS.
HAH
MYA

JUST IN CASE,
PUT THIS ON HER, TOO.

WHA ?
WHAT... IS THAT ?
WHA ?!
MEOWR
WHAT IS THIS?!
I'M HOME !
AH ! SO ...
WHAT DID THEY SAY?
SHE SHOULD BE FINE WITH EYEDROPS.
MEDICINE
I HOPE SHE GETS WELL SOON.
WEL-COME BACK, CHI.
POP
I'M HOME!
FWING
WHA ?!

FWING
HUH ?
CHI LOOKS WEIRD !
IT'S CALLED AN ELIZ-ABETHAN COL-LAR.
IT'S USED TO PREVENT HER FROM RUBBING HER EYE.
...
AH
GOOD IDEA.
MOOT
MOOT
MOOT
MOOT
TURN
TURN
DADDY, I CAN'T TAKE THIS THING OFF!
MEOW
TAKE IT OFF FOR ME!
MEOW

GOOD GIRL.
PAT PAT
WHAT?!
OH, THE ITCHIES ...
ZING ZING
HEY?
SKEF SKEF SKEF SKEF
MEOW
HEY?
AH, IT DOES GUARD HER EYES.
I CAN'T REACH!
MEOW
GOOD IDEA.
SKEF SKEF SKEF SKEF
HAH~
HUH HUH HUH

CHI'S HUNGRY
AND THIRSTY.
TIP
TIP
TIP
EVEN WHEN SHE GETS BETTER, SHE'LL STAY HOME AT FIRST.
YEAH.
FOOD, FOOD.
TIP TIP TIP
KLUNK
MYA
HUH?
HMM?
MEOW
A RUDE SURPRISE ...
TIP TIP TIP...

KLUNK
MYA
HEY?
CHI'S BUMPING INTO THINGS EVERY-WHERE SHE WALKS.
?
WHAT'S GOING ON?
SHE'S YET TO FATHOM HER NEW WIDTH.
WELL, IT DID CHANGE SUD-DENLY.
MEOW
HEY ?
ZZASH
MEOW
HMMM ?
SKRFF
HUH?
YOU HOPE TO GET THROUGH THAT?
TIP
TIP
TIP

WHAM
MEOW
I CAN'T GET THROUGH!
THERE'S NO WAY, CHI.
GOT IT?
YOINK
HA

TIP TIP TIP TIP

OH, CHI, THAT TOO

MIGHT NOT WORK...

MEEEE
I CAN'T EAT!!

the end

Extra

Chi's Sweet Origami!

Let's Make a Chi Face!!

Copy or cut out the image to the right and fold using the following instructions.

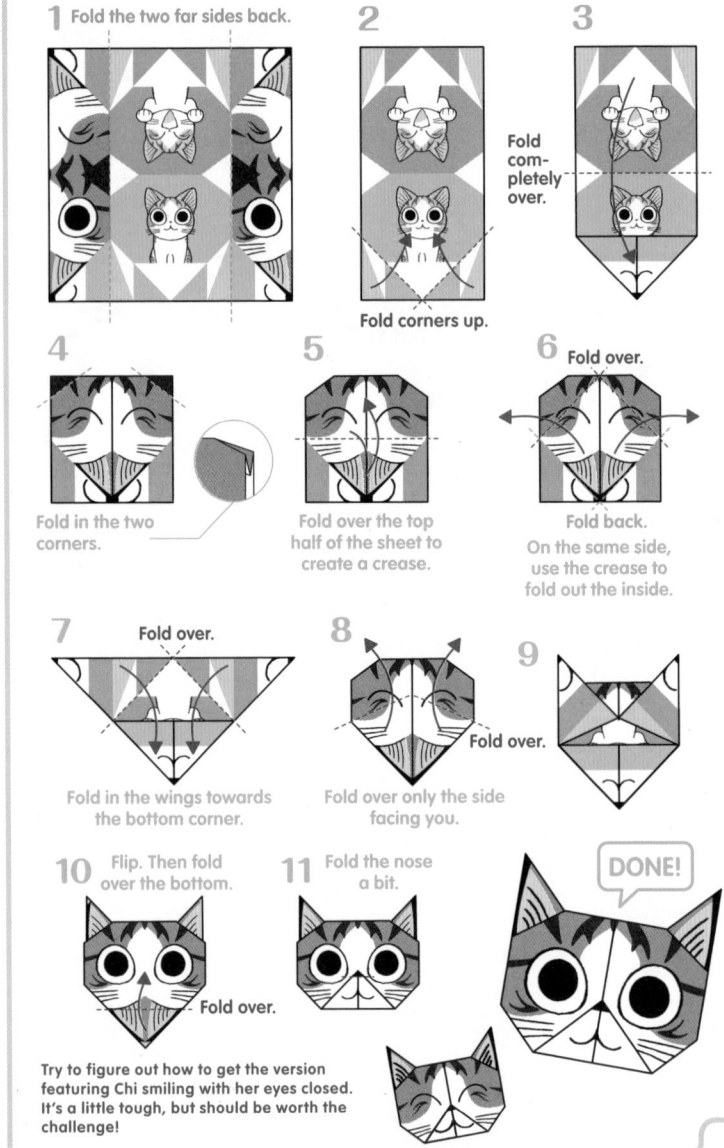

Try to figure out how to get the version featuring Chi smiling with her eyes closed. It's a little tough, but should be worth the challenge!

Origami (instructions on facing page)

Let's try to fold our way to both of Chi's origami faces!

Chi's Sweet Home volume 9
Available Now!

Chi's Sweet Home, volume 8

Translation - Ed Chavez
Production - Hiroko Mizuno
Tomoe Tsutsumi

Copyright © 2012 Konami Kanata. All rights reserved.
First published in Japan in 2011 by Kodansha, Ltd., Tokyo
Publication for this English edition arranged through Kodansha, Ltd., Tokyo
English language version produced by Vertical, Inc.

Translation provided by Vertical, Inc., 2012
Published by Vertical, Inc., New York

Originally published in Japanese as *Chiizu Suiito Houmu* by Kodansha, Ltd., 2009-2010
Chiizu Suiito Houmu first serialized in *Morning*, Kodansha, Ltd., 2004-

This is a work of fiction.

ISBN: 978-1-935654-35-3

Manufactured in China

First Edition

Second Printing

Vertical, Inc.
451 Park Avenue South, 7th Floor
New York, NY 10016
www.vertical-inc.com

5490035

Special thanks to: K. Kitamoto

A12006 370339

homemade 132: a cat is wowed

MEOW
MOVE
MRR
IN MY WAY!
MRR
WHAT?!
MEOW
STOP!

IT'S NO GOOD.
MEOW
MRR
LET'S DO THIS AGAIN.
TAP
TAP

WE CAN'T GO THROUGH TOGETHER.
MIYA
MRR
LOOKS LIKE IT.

MRR
WE'VE GOTTA GO THROUGH ONE BY ONE.

YUP, YOU'RE RIGHT.
MRR

SQU EEZ

CHI'S GOING IN FIRST!
MEOW
MRR
NO, I AM!
MERR
OF COURSE I'M GOING FIRST!